ELEMENTARY MINI LESSONS

Suzette!
Thanks for
sharing in my
joy for writing!
God Bless,
Jodi Ramos.
(210) 695-9998
Jodi_Ramos@nisd.net

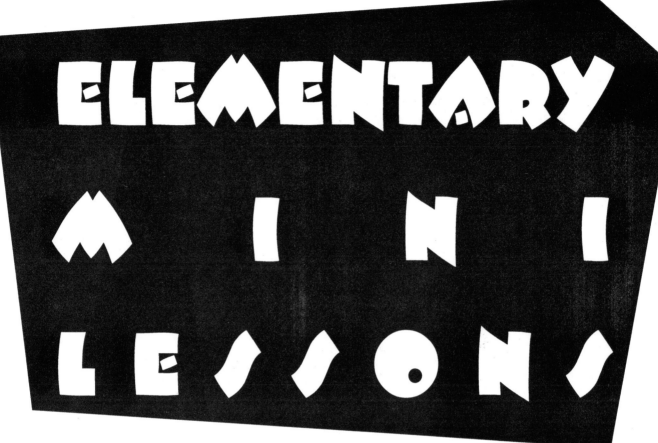

ELEMENTARY MINI LESSONS

Lessons and songs,
to motivate, inspire,
and improve writing skills

JODI RAMOS

Absey & Co.

"That is question now;
And then comes answer like an Absey book.
King John, 1, 1
Shakespeare

Dedication
To my three m & m's- Merrick Miguel, Malaeni Marie and Marina May.
You make each day sweet and satisfying.
J.R.

Requests for permission to make copies
of the text of the work should be mailed to:
Permissions
Absey & Co. Inc.
23011 Northcrest
Spring, Texas 77389

ISBN 1-88842-20-2

ELEMENTARY MINILESSONS

TABLE OF CONTENTS

Acknowledgements
Format Introduction

TABLE OF CONTENTS

Acknowledgments

This book would never have been completed without the many requests to publish from my colleagues in the New Jersey Writing Project in Texas, my principal Pat Cerutti, friends and family members.

To Rita Kay Driggers, a librarian to be inspired by;

To Aunt Ruth and Aunt Cece, two ladies I will always hold in my heart;

To Randy, whose voice I still hear;

To Lisa Parsons, who had the courage to read my handwriting and type it as well;

To Natalie Adams, for her illustrations and courage;

To Leslie Iakovides, Joy Moore, and Twyla Kessler who exemplify the statement *forever a friend*;

To Paula Warden and Barbara Edens, my calm workshop partners;

To Joyce and Trey, for giving me the opportunity to share;

To Mrs. Roberts' 4th grade class for giving this book a thumbs up;

To the staff and students at Steubing Elementary who let me try my ideas out on them;

To my husband, who lets me be me;

To David and Susie Meyers—parent volunteers who never stop giving;

To my Father in Heaven whose strength sustains me.

FORMAT INTRODUCTION

Elementary Minilessons have all or at least one of three major components:
Motivation

Songs

Petunia, a puppet

The lessons are designed to be worked into the curriculum as students need them. All the lessons are created to aid the instructor in teaching writing as a process. They are to enhance the prewriting, writing, revising, editing and publishing that goes on throughout the year.

The words to the songs were composed to attract the students' attention, giving them an easy way to remember important parts of the writing process. According to Newsweek, *Music excites the inherent brain patterns and enhances their use in complex reasoning tasks. Music trains the brain for higher forms of thinking.* ("Your Child's Brain," *Newsweek*, February 1998.)

The puppet was used because behind every great teacher is a great imagination. Petunia has been a part of my imagination for my entire teaching career. She helps me teach each lesson and has even earned superior ratings from my principals. Petunia's picture will be in some of the lessons holding a prop. Petunia is easily confused, and the students teach her as they learn about each element.

Petunia and her home.

ELEMENTARY MINILESSONS

#1

Crackling and Crunching— Your Way through Four Genre!

(These lessons can be taught consecutively or separately as you teach each type of writing)

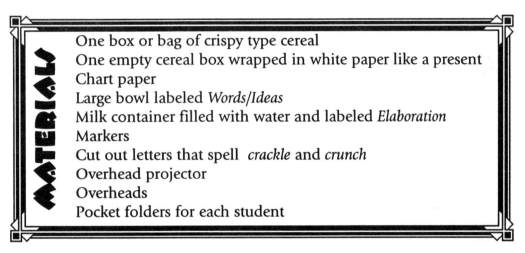

MATERIALS

One box or bag of crispy type cereal
One empty cereal box wrapped in white paper like a present
Chart paper
Large bowl labeled *Words/Ideas*
Milk container filled with water and labeled *Elaboration*
Markers
Cut out letters that spell *crackle* and *crunch*
Overhead projector
Overheads
Pocket folders for each student

Motivation:

Day One :

• Take out wrapped cereal box and glue the characters *Crackle* and *Crunch* and side inserts as shown on pages 47-51.

• Talk to the students about their writing. Explain that their papers often start out superbly but then fizzle out. They do not keep crackling and crunching to the end. Remind students that good writing has elaboration and voice. Their writing should crackle with vivid verbs and precise adjectives, from beginning to end. Their writing should also crunch with their specific voices. For example, the crunch of an apple sounds different than the crunch of footsteps through snow.

• Fill the bowl labeled *Words/Ideas* with a cup or two of cereal.

• Pour water from the jug labeled *Elaboration* into the bowl. Be careful not to add too much elaboration or the writing will become soggy.

• Listen to the *Words* and *Ideas* crackle and crunch

• Walk the bowl around to each student. The crackle sound will begin to soften.

• Guide students to discover that more elaboration is needed. Add more water (elaboration) from the jug.

• Guide students to discover that excessive elaboration doesn't work either. Add more crispy cereal (words/ideas) to the bowl. Discuss how a good writer continually adds words and ideas mixed with elaboration.

• Challenge the students to envision themselves crunching into a bowl of corn crispers. Whose crunch would be the loudest?

• Show the box of *Corn Crispers* to the students. Making an overhead of each side may be easier for large groups of students to see.

• Discuss how *Crackle* and *Crunch* will show them four different types of writing. They will be asked to help *Crackle* and *Crunch* with a type of writing each day of the week ,keeping in mind that they must crackle and crunch throughout their papers.

• Students should take a pocket folder and write *Crackle* and *Crunch* on its cover in about two inch letters. They will need this folder to hold their ideas throughout the week and have it available throughout the year.

Day two:

• Show students the side of the box that has the recipe for Crackle Pops on it.

• Discuss what makes a good *How-To* piece of writing. (See Mini lessons # 8 and 9 for more ideas.)

• Read the directions; and if possible make a batch of Crackle Pops.

• Discuss each part of Crackle's recipe. Use a chart paper or an overhead to record major points. The recipe does a good job but how could the beginning and end be made better?

✓ Were the directions easy to follow?

✓ Does anything need to be added to make the process clearer?

✓ Does the recipe use sequence words?

✓ Is there a better way to organize the paragraph?

✓ Point out that Crackle used her voice, *"They are named after me but you can make them too." "This is the tricky part."* Could *Crackle* have used voice more often? Stress that even though Crackle did a great job she can always do better.

Day three:

• Show the students the side of the box that states the comparison and contrasting of corn crispers with skim milk and without. Crunch doesn't finish his piece of writing. He needs the student's help. Point out the good things about Crunch's writing and also brainstorm what he could have done better. Then challenge the students to finish the piece of writing. After they finish comparing and contrasting, have them share what they wrote.

• Or, as a class write an ending that fits with *Crunch's* beginning.

Day four:

• Show the students the back of the box. It has a letter. *Crackle* and *Crunch* give three reasons why people should buy corn crispers and invite the students to help them write persuasively.

• Guide the students to put *Crackle* and *Crunch's* reasons in the best order or change the reasons as *Crunch* suggests. Students work in groups, but they work as a class to add an appropriate beginning and ending.

- Students are always welcome to share their writing.

Day five:

- Show students the cover of the box with Crackle and Crunch in a bowl of corn crispers.

- Discuss the elements of a narrative(story). (See mini lesson 12 for more ideas.)

- Invite students to write a story about *Crackle* and *Crunch*. Take out the bowl used in Day One and again fill with crispy cereal. Walk around reminding them to crackle and crunch throughout their writing. Next put up the large chart, as shown below. (I usually tape it to my map and roll it down when I reach this point.)

C	hildren
R	emember
A	nd
C	arefully
K	eep
L	ovingly
E	laborating!

C	hildren
R	emember
U	se what you
k N	ow!
C	hildren
s H	ow!

Point out that these letters could stand for types of writing/elaboration.

C	ompare
R	pe
A	djectives
C	
K	
a L	literation
E	

C	ontrast
R	suade
U	
N	arrative
C	ontrast
meta H	ors

Enlist students to help fill in the chart. The possibilities are endless!

ELEMENTARY MINILESSONS

• If your school takes a standardized test, share with other faculty members that *C C* stands for *Children Can*. Ask them to say, "*C C*" when students who take the test come by. On test day dress up a student in corn crispers boxes and have them walk the halls as motivation for those taking the test.

• Teach students the following chant while *Crackle* and *Crunch* strut their stuff.

Today is the day to be the best you can be!
Take it slow , use all you know
And the writing will surely flow!
    Similes, adjectives, metaphors and more—
    Readers are in for a treat that's for sure!
    C C means that children can—
Just stick to your creative plan.
Remember to crackle and crunch along the way ,
the readers will score your paper a three or a four, which will
surely make your day!
    CC   CC   CC   CC
    Children Can!!!!!!!!

ELEMENTARY MINILESSONS

MINILESSON #2 — Similes to Smile About

MATERIALS

Stuffed animal or puppet
A large paper smile
Quick as a Cricket, Audrey Wood
White paper
Construction paper
Individual class picture (the kind you receive when students photos are taken.)
Copy of *Elaboration* song (page 39)

Motivation:

• Show your stuffed animal or puppet to the class.

• Tell the students that your friend (the puppet or stuffed animal) thinks that *simile* means to *smile.*

• Explain to the class that they will learn about similes and put the smile on the puppet's face. A simile is a figure of speech where two items are compared using *like* or *as.* Sing the Elaboration Song (see p 59)and discover the simile.

• Read *Quick as a Cricket* to show more examples of similes.

• Brainstorm other similes.

• Students write and illustrate a simile about themselves.

• Hand out the individual pictures for students to use in their illustration. Students can affix their photo to a concrete object and then write a simile comparing themselves to the object. Students can also create a drawing and glue their photo onto the drawing. Example: One student glued her picture to a soda can then she wrote. *Bailey is as bubbly as a soda.*

• Bind the similes and illustrations into a class book or display their 3D similes in the school library.

• Challenge the students to add a simile into their current piece of writing.

ELEMENTARY MINILESSONS

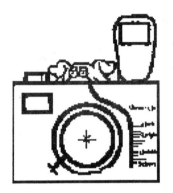

MINILESSON

#3

Delight Them With Details

MATERIALS

Camera handout (page 52)
Construction paper (one sheet per child or index cards or both)
Push pin

Motivation:

• Provide each student with a faux camera and construction paper or students may draw a camera on a blank index card.

• Students cut out their camera or glue the faux camera to construction paper and cut it out.

• The teacher pokes a hole with the pushpin in the center of the camera.

• Each student finds an object in the room by looking through the view finder in the camera. (You will be amazed at how much you see.)

• After studying the object, students write a description. Then they move closer and add as many details as possible.

• Model the use of adding details by orally describing what you see or by writing what you see on an overhead transparency or on butcher paper.

• One by one the students share their descriptions while classmates attempt to guess the object.

• Discuss the importance of details in their writing. Have them look at a paper that they are working on and add details where needed.

#4 Alliteration Galore

MATERIALS

Two letters of the alphabet per child
(I use contact paper purchased from the grocery store
or discount store to punch my letters from. They stick
easily onto walls, folders, books.)
Z Was Zapped, Chris Van Allsburg
Animalia, Graeme Base

Motivation:

• Tape or stick the letters all over the classroom. Read the *Z Was Zapped* or *Animalia* and discuss alliteration. Alliteration occurs when two or more words in a sentence have the same beginning sound.

• Model choosing a letter such as B.
Example: Bobby bought blue balloons because Billy's blue balloon broke.
Each child takes two letters from around the room and writes an alliterative sentence for each letter. (If you teach young children you may want to encourage them to take letters other than X and Z.)

• The students glue their letters on the paper and illustrate their sentences.

• Encourage them to go back into their current writing piece and add some alliteration.
Note: *The Z Was Zapped* is also good for encouraging the use of adverbs and horizontal elaboration. Remind the students that Chris Van Allsburg definitely knows how to elaborate. He does not say F was flattened, instead he says, *F was firmly flattened*.
He does not say B was bitten. He says, *B was badly bitten*.

MINILESSON

#5 Sentence Combining

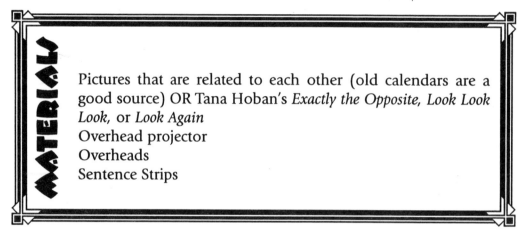

MATERIALS

Pictures that are related to each other (old calendars are a good source) OR Tana Hoban's *Exactly the Opposite, Look Look Look,* or *Look Again*
Overhead projector
Overheads
Sentence Strips

Motivation:

• Make separate overheads of two pictures or display two pictures from one of the books.

• Divide the class in half. Show the first picture to the class. Half the class, working as a group, writes a sentence about what they see.

• Show the other picture to the class. The other half of the class, working as a group, writes a sentence about that picture.

• Ask a student from each group to share the group's sentence. Write each sentence on a transparency or butcher paper for all to see.

• Ask volunteers to combine the two sentences. Discuss how sentences can be combined: Suggest conjunctions, semi colons, and transitional phrases. Repeat the activity with different pictures.

• This works well with pairs of students who work independently and then share how they combined their sentences.

• Give each pair a sentence strip. Pairs will combine their sentences and write the combined sentence on the sentence strip. After the sentence is shared orally, it can be posted.

• Remember to have the students go back into their current writing and strive to combine some of their short choppy sentences into longer ones.

MINILESSON #6

Creating Your Writing Community Atmosphere

MATERIALS

Author, Helen Lester
One box (any shape or size)
Copy of song *Writing the _____ Way,* (your school's name goes in the blank) (page 40)

Motivation:

- Read *Author* to the students, preferably with them around you on the floor.
- Discuss the fizzle box that Lester uses in the story.
- Divide the class into four groups. Each group decorates one side of the box. Using construction paper, markers, crayons, and so forth..
- Explain that this box will be used to hold writing that the students would normally throw away. Perhaps the student started a story but it just didn't work. Or, a student wrote three beginnings but only will use one. These writings are no longer needed, yet another student may find them useful.
- When brainstorming topics, modeling a type of writing ,or writing a class story remember to write on butcher paper and also place it in the box.
- When a student says, *I don't know what to write about*, direct them to the fizzle box.
- Someone else's trash may be their treasure!
- Sing , *Writing the _____ Way* , reminding students that there are stages to writing and that writing is a process.

ELEMENTARY MINILESSONS

#1 *How To Know How**

MATERIALS

Vanilla wafers (two per student)
Chocolate peppermint patties (one per student)
Decorating gel in red and yellow (found in the cake decorating section of the supermarket)
Shredded coconut (plain)
Shredded coconut dyed green (Shake food coloring and coconut together in a baggy.)
Sesame seeds (optional)
The Sensational Samburger, David Pelham
Overhead projector or chalkboard

Motivation:

- Read *The Sensational Samburger* or discuss a time that they ate hamburgers.
- Put this list on the board or overhead:

Cookies = buns	Yellow gel = mustard	Mint = patty
Red gel = Ketchup	Green coconut = lettuce	Sesame seeds
Plain coconut = onions		

- Students create their own *hamburger* using the materials you provided. (The sesame seeds may be applied to a moistened cookie to resemble a sesame seed bun.)
- Students write down the steps they went through in creating their own *hamburger*. They can do this as they build their burgers or when they are finished.
- After the steps are listed, discuss the importance of a good introduction and conclusion.
- On butcher paper, write an introduction and conclusion as a class. Stress context.
- Students should write their own introduction and conclusion.
- Students take turns sharing. Discuss the importance of good sequence words and specific details.

* The author presented a minilesson workshop asking teachers to bring an idea of their own. Myrna Glikman presented the idea for this lesson.

ELEMENTARY MINILESSONS

8 S u c c e s s f u l Sequence Words

(For writing a *How To*)

MINILESSON

MATERIALS

> Pencil sharpener dot-to-dot (page 53)
> *The How To Song* (page 41)

Motivation:

- As a class brainstorm sequence or transition words.
  Examples: first, second, third, then, next, furthermore, finally, and so forth
- Pass out dot-to-dot pages. On each number have the students write a transition word.
  Examples: (. 1) first, (. 2) second, (. 3) third, (. 4) next, etc.
- Using an overhead of the dot - to - dot helps guide students and provides a good model.
- Students connect the dots to reveal the pencil sharpener.
- They should keep this tool in their writing folders to use when writing a *How To* paper.
- Sing the *How To Song* as a reminder to use sequence/transition words.
- Encourage the students to check their current piece of writing for appropriate transition words.

ELEMENTARY MINILESSONS

MINILESSON #9

More *How-To* Writing

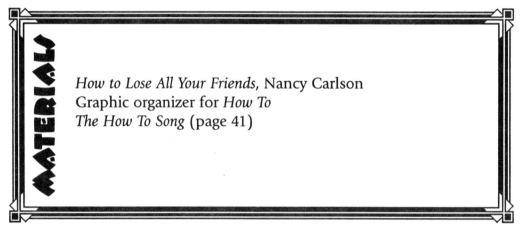

MATERIALS

How to Lose All Your Friends, Nancy Carlson
Graphic organizer for *How To*
The How To Song (page 41)

Motivation:

- Read *How to Lose All Your Friends*.
- Discuss each step and how it is elaborated.
- Write down each step on butcher paper including the introduction and conclusion. Do this together as a class activity. Discuss the importance of writing an introduction and conclusion that fits the writing.
- Sing *How To Song* as a reminder to use sequence words.
- Students work individually or in pairs rewriting the story as, *How to keep your friends.*
- Students share their *How-To's* and display them along with the book in the classroom or in the library.
- Encourage students to go into their *How-To* piece and check for clear steps and a solid introduction conclusion.

ELEMENTARY MINILESSONS

How To Graphic Organizer

Introduction in Context

First ,
Second,
Third,
Fourth,
Fifth,
Sixth,
Seventh,

Conclusion in context

ELEMENTARY MINILESSONS

MINILESSON

#10 Run-On Sentences

MATERIALS

One long strip of paper about six inches wide or colorful sentence strips taped around the classroom. (Cash register tape works too.)
A run-on sentence about your students. Each student should be named individually in the sentence.

Motivation:

• Before the students arrive, write a long run-on sentence about your students on the paper strip.

Example: The teacher watched as Mary and Robert walked into the classroom they looked a little sleepy then Margaret, Sue and Joy entered....

• Display it around the room at eye level for the students.

• When writing the sentence do not capitalize words that begin the sentence. This would make it too easy for the students to figure out where the sentences start and end.

• When the students enter the classroom, instruct them to take out their journals and copy the sentence as is.

• Together, read the sentence. Talk about it as a run-on sentence. Discuss how to correct the run-on using capitalization and punctuation.

• Students make corrections on their own copy as you correct the displayed run-on the wall.

• Encourage students to look at their current writing.

• Volunteers call out the run-on sentences from their pieces as you write them on the overhead.

• Guide them as a class to correct the run-on sentences.

ELEMENTARY MINILESSONS

MINILESSON

#11

Who? What? When? Where? Why? & How?

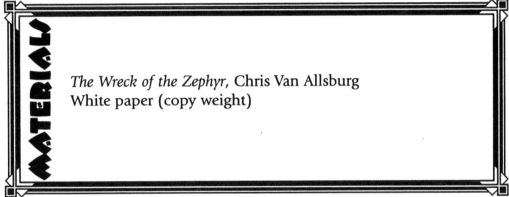

MATERIALS

The Wreck of the Zephyr, Chris Van Allsburg
White paper (copy weight)

Motivation:

• Read the *Wreck of the Zephyr* to the students. The ending of this story challenge students to discover the narrator.

• Use the following questions to guide students as they discuss the story: Who was telling the story? What hint did the author of the book give you?

• Discuss the Reporter's Formula. These are questions that good reporters ask before they write up their story. Who? What? When? Where? Why? How?

• Make a paper boat (see direction on the following pages)

• Draw a little man on the top of the sail (triangle). Stick figures are fine.

Tell the following story: A man is sailing on a sunny day. Along comes a storm. (Make storm noises with a CD or pots and pans.) The storm damages one side of the boat. (Tear one.) The storm ruins the other side. (Tear two). Finally the storm washes up to the top of the sail. (Tear three.) The people look and look and all they find is the gentleman's T-shirt. (Open the boat to find a T-shirt.) Do not to fear because the Red Cross is near! (Open it up again to find a cross.)

• Elaborate the story differently each time.

For example, sometimes the boat hits an iceberg or is attacked by pirates. Just remember to tear the boat in the correct places.

• Instruct the students to make their own boat and write a story describing the who,

ELEMENTARY MINILESSONS

what, when, where, why, and how of their boat adventure.

- Share.

- Encourage the students to reenter their current piece of writing. They check to see that their stories include who, what, when, where, why, and how.

- Make a grid to keep track of the elements. On top of a piece of notebook paper have them write Who, What, When, Where, Why, and How or see chart following this lesson.

- Students fill in their grids as they check their piece of writing for Who, What, When, Where, Why, and How.

Did you use the reporter's formula in your writing?					
Who ?	What ?	When ?	Where ?	Why ?	How ?

ELEMENTARY MINILESSONS

Directions for boat:

1. Fold a 8 1/2″ x 11″ piece of paper in half. Short end to short end

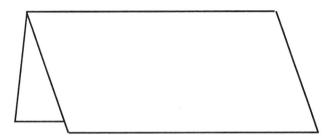

2. With fold at top, fold each side in to create two triangles.

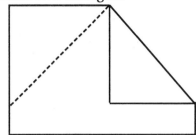

3. Fold up flaps on both side of the bottom.

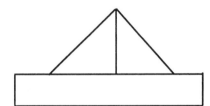

4. Tear one.

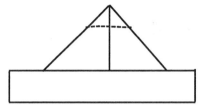

5. Tear two.

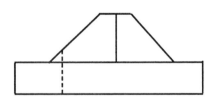

6. Tear three.

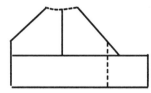

7. Open to T-shirt.

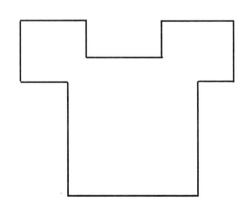

8. Open to cross.

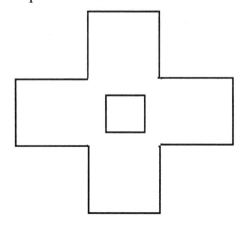

ELEMENTARY MINILESSONS

MINILESSON #12   Elements of a Narrative

MATERIALS

Small plastic gloves (Custodians are a great resource.)
Permanent marker
I've Got The Whole Story In My Hands song (page 41-42)
Aunt Isabell Tells a Good One, Kate Duke

Motivation:

This lesson is modeled after Helen Van Cott's 1996 NJWPT recertification, *Elaboration as a Model*, in Austin, Texas 1997.

• Read *Aunt Isabell Tells a Good One*.

• As a class list the elements of a good story: setting, characters, events, problem, and solution. Discuss these elements as they are given in the book.

• Students take the plastic glove and with a permanent marker write one element on each finger and the word *Elaboration* on the palm. (see illustration).

• Students should wear their gloves as they check their current piece of writing to ensure that they included the elements of a narrative. Making a grid would be helpful. Students can make their own grid.

• Sing *I've Got the Whole Story in My Hand* to reinforce the concept.

ELEMENTARY MINILESSONS

#13 LEADS/ Beginnings

MATERIALS

3 sticky notes for each student

Motivation:

• Read the leads(the first two sentences) in a variety of the students' favorite books. Try to find one lead with action, one with dialogue, and one that makes an exclamatory statement. Here are some examples:

Whooooooo! from **"Uh Oh!" said the Crow**

Late one night as I sat reading I heard the sound of feeding. from **Pigs Aplenty, Pigs Galore**,

Hello my name is Janet Stevens, and I am an illustrator . Drawing pictures for books is my job. Authors write words. Then I do the artwork. Psst. Psst. Ja-a-a-anet What? Who's there? from **Pictures to Words** by Janet Stevens

• Discuss the three leads. Tell the students that they have twenty seconds to capture the reader's interest. You have to encourage the reader read on.

• Write . "" ! on the board. I tell the students to write three new beginnings for their current piece of writing.

• Pass out sticky notes.

• The students write one dialogue ("") lead, one exclamation (!) lead, and one action(.) lead on each sticky note!

• Students read their three leads. Students may want to vote on the one that best captures the reader's attention. Thumbs up meaning the best , thumbs down for the worst lead and thumbs sideways for an ok lead.

• Students write down how many chose lead number one as the best and plot it on a bar graph. They do the same for lead number two and three. You can do one child's bar graph on the board as an example.

ELEMENTARY MINILESSONS

MINILESSON #14 Endings

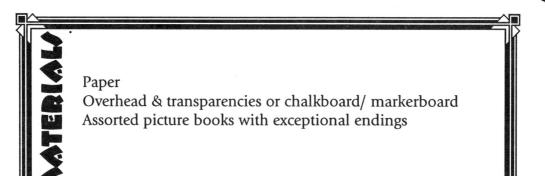

Paper
Overhead & transparencies or chalkboard/ markerboard
Assorted picture books with exceptional endings

Motivation:

• Draw three animals without tails on the board or overhead.
Examples might include a cat, a dog, and a horse.

• Ask the students to tell you what is missing.

• When they determine that the tail is missing, draw a pig's curly tail on the cat.
As they shout, *No!* change the tail and remind them that their pieces need an ending that fits the story.

• Read the endings of some favorite picture books.

• Discuss the endings. Why are they good. Be sure to include some examples that fit the context well.

• Brainstorm what makes a good ending: gives the reader something to think about, concludes the falling action or ties the story together.

• Students reenter their stories and write two different endings.

• Students share endings with a partner and chose the one they want to use to conclude their story!

ELEMENTARY MINILESSONS

#15 Compare & Contrast

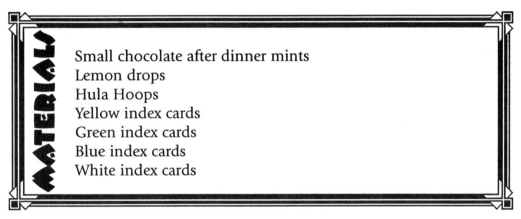

MATERIALS

Small chocolate after dinner mints
Lemon drops
Hula Hoops
Yellow index cards
Green index cards
Blue index cards
White index cards

Motivation:

• Give each student one lemon drop and one yellow index card.
• Students look, feel, smell and taste the lemon drop.
• They write three sentences on the yellow index card describing the lemon drop.
• Give each child one small chocolate after-dinner mint and a green card.
• Students look, feel, smell and taste the mint.
• They write three sentences on the green index card describing the small chocolate after-dinner mint.
• Next give each child one blue index card. On this card students write how the lemon drop and mint are alike.
• Give each child one white index card. On this card students write how the lemon drop and mint are different.
• Place the Hula-Hoops on the floor like the circles of a Venn Diagram.
• Have the students place the cards in specific areas of the Hula-Hoop. In the left circle place the descriptions of the small chocolate after-dinner mints. In the right circle place the descriptions of the lemon drops. In .the intersection of the hoops place the similarities. Under the circles place the differences.
• Discuss what is in a good compare and contrast paper.
• Look at the students' current compare and contrast papers and encourage them to add more items about each side.

ELEMENTARY MINILESSONS

#16 Dialogue*

MATERIALS

Macaroni noodles
Food coloring
Rubbing alcohol
Plastic bags
Any *Amelia Bedelia* book by Peggy Parish
Prior to the lesson, dye the noodles by placing equal parts alcohol and food coloring in a bag with the noodles. After the process is complete place the noodles out to dry.

Motivation:

• Read a page or two from *Amelia Bedelia*.

• Discuss the way an author shows that a character is speaking.

• Discuss quotation marks and compare to the shape of lips. Quotation marks go around what is said just like our lips go around what we say. The opening " shows a person beginning to speak; the closing " shows the person has stopped speaking.

• Students reenter one of their current pieces of writing and add dialogue between two of their characters.

• Students search for dialogue in their writing, and put *two lips* around what their characters say.

• Students use the macaroni noodles as the quotation marks. Just as we have two lips they should use two noodles for each quotation mark. They glue the noodles right on their paper in the proper places.

• Students add the dialogue that they wrote into their story.

• Encourage students to add dialogue if they do not have any in their current writing.

• Students share.

*Based on a lesson by Kelley Smith

ELEMENTARY MINILESSONS

MINILESSON

#11

More Dialogu

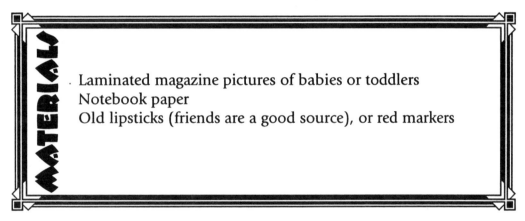

MATERIALS

Laminated magazine pictures of babies or toddlers
Notebook paper
Old lipsticks (friends are a good source), or red markers

Motivation:

• Pass out one baby picture to each student or pair of students.

• Ask students to write down what the baby would say if he/she could. After the students have finished writing, give them a lipstick or marker to put the *two lips* (quotation marks) around what was said.

• Remind them that quotation marks go around what was said just as our lips around what we say.

• Students check the piece of writing that they are working on to see if they used quotation marks correctly.

• Students check to make certain they closed their quotation marks.

• Encourage the use of dialogue as a form of elaboration.

ELEMENTARY MINILESSONS

MINILESSON #18 Using the Sense of Sight

MATERIALS

Chart paper with 5 senses written on the top:
Seeing   Smelling   Hearing   Tasting   Touching
An individual sense chart for each child
If You Were a Writer, Joan Lowery Nixon
Yellow acetate
3 Sheets of 8 1/2" x 11" paper

Motivation:

• Read page six of *If You Were a Writer.* (The pages are not numbered in the book, so for ease of reference, I started numbering them after the dedication page.)

• Discuss the words that the girl uses in the book as she looks at the sunset. Using an overhead create a sunset on a transparency. Cover the glass on an overhead projector with yellow acetate. Secure with tape. Cut out a circle or sun image from the middle of a 8 1/2 by 11 sheet of paper, then extend the paper by stapling an extra sheet of paper to its bottom or top. This covers the yellow acetate (except for the circle/sun) and allow you to slowly pull the circle up and down thereby creating a sunrise and sunset.

• Write the students' responses to the sunset/sunrise and the sensory words from the book under the word *sight* on the large chart for the class.

• Students go to a window and write down on their individual sense chart what they see.

• Share descriptions that use the senses from books you read to the students.

• Encourage students to use the sense of sight in their current piece of writing.

ELEMENTARY MINILESSONS

MINILESSON #19 — Using the Sense of Smell

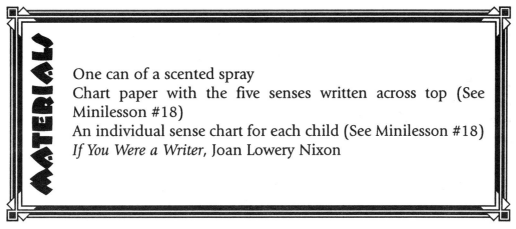

MATERIALS

One can of a scented spray
Chart paper with the five senses written across top (See Minilesson #18)
An individual sense chart for each child (See Minilesson #18)
If You Were a Writer, Joan Lowery Nixon

Motivation:

- Read the sentences on page four that describe the smell of apple pie. The pages are not numbered in the book, so for ease of reference, I began numbering them after the dedication page.
- Cut several apples into pieces and have the students describe the aroma.
- Write the words from the book and the students' responses describing the smell of the apples on the class chart under the word *smelling*.
- Spray the scented spray all over the room.
- Students write the *smell words* the air freshener evokes on their individual charts.
- Students reenter their current writing piece and look for opportunities to use their sense of smell.
- Encourage students to share their work, especially their *smell words*.

ELEMENTARY MINILESSONS

#20 Using the Sense of Sound

MATERIALS

Chart paper with the five senses written across top (See Minilesson #18)
An individual sense chart for each child (See Minilesson #18)
If You Were a Writer, Joan Lowery Nixon
A tape of sounds recorded in and around your refrigerator
A tape player

Motivation:

• Show students page 22. The pages are not numbered in the book, so for ease of reference, I began numbering them after the dedication page.

• Discuss the bear's exploration of the refrigerator. Tell students to listen to a tape you made of your son or daughter or puppet's exploration of your refrigerator. Make sure to tape the opening and closing of the door, the opening of a milk jug, ketchup bottle, cracking an egg, slicing cheese, crunching an apple, peeling an orange, shredding of lettuce, opening a soda can and any other interesting sounds.

• Discuss the sounds heard and what the bear in the book heard.

• Write the sound words under the word *hearing* on the chart.

• Students add these sensory words to their individual charts.

• Encourage the students to use the sound words in their writing.

ELEMENTARY MINILESSONS

MINILESSON #21 Using the Sense of Taste

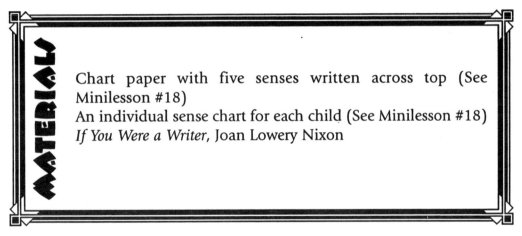

MATERIALS

Chart paper with five senses written across top (See Minilesson #18)
An individual sense chart for each child (See Minilesson #18)
If You Were a Writer, Joan Lowery Nixon

Motivation:

• Read page 18 where Melia eats a peanut butter and strawberry jam sandwich. There is no description of the taste in the book. The pages are not numbered in the book, so for ease of reference, I began numbering them after the dedication page.

• Students infer what the sandwich might taste like. Write their inferences under the word *tasting* on the chart.

• Instruct the students to take out their individual sense chart and fill up the column under *tasting* with tasty words.

• Bake something with strawberries (and have the class eat it and describe what it tasted like) or bring in strawberry candy , jelly beans, wafer cookies or licorice to be tasted.

• Encourage students to use the sense of taste in their current piece of writing.

ELEMENTARY MINILESSONS

#22 Using the Sense of Touch

MATERIAL

Chart paper with five senses written on top (See Motivation #18)
Individual sense chart for each child (See Motivation #18)
If You Were a Writer, Joan Lowery Nixon
4 bags or boxes with different items for the students to touch

Motivation:

• Read the section of page four that describes the little girl feeling her uncle's beard. The pages are not numbered in the book, so for ease of reference, I began numbering them after the dedication page.

  • Write those *touch* words under the word *touching* on the chart.

  • Pass around the bags or boxes. Students feel what is inside without peeking.

  • Students write down the *touch* words on their individual sense charts.

  • Encourage students to use the sense of touch in their current writing.

ELEMENTARY MINILESSONS

MINILESSON #23 — Triptych Prewriting

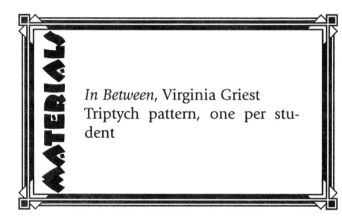

In Between, Virginia Griest
Triptych pattern, one per student

Motivation:

- Read *In Between*
- Discuss the beginning, middle and end.
- Explain that triptych comes from ancient, hinged, three sectioned tablets or three-paneled tapestries. See *Acts of Teaching*, page 195.
- Students create their own triptych by securing several sheets of paper together and stapling it across its top. (They may also use three brads across the top to secure the pages.)

Head	Body	Tail
Noun phrase or name of animal	Verb or verb phrase	Prepositional phrase where or what

- Students cut the paper vertically in two places to create three columns.
- They fill in the pages by drawing the head, body, and tail of an animal.
- Then they write in the appropriate column a noun phrase or the animal's name, a verb or verb phrase, and a prepositional phrase that tells where or when.
- Students flip sections to create new animals and new sentences.
- Encourage students to flip through their writing to see if some sentences can be changed by adding noun, verb, or prepositional phrases.

ELEMENTARY MINILESSONS

#24 Horizontal Elaboration*

MATERIALS

Elaboration cards (see page 55) laminated or made into a transparency
An overhead projector (if transparency is used above)
One simple sentence

Motivation:

- Cut out cards and place them in a stack.
- Display a simple sentence on the overhead or the board.
    Example: The cat played.
- Students draw a card from the stack.
- Students add a word or words asked for on the card.
    Example: The student draws a *what* card. The cat played. (What?) The cat played hide and seek.
- Continue playing until the class completes the sentence as best they can. Blank cards can be used for whatever you want them to add.
    Examples: a specific form of speech, a verb, or a prepositional phrase
The wild card lets students add anything they want.
- Let student's imagination guide them to the many ways that their game can be used. The possibilities are unlimited.
- Have students look at their current piece of writing and check for unelaborated sentences. Put some of the sentences on the board and play the game to elaborate.
- Have students play the game in partners with unelaborated sentences from their current piece of writing.
    *The idea for this lesson came from Jean Gage.

ELEMENTARY MINILESSONS

MINILESSON

#25 Vertical Elaboration*

MATERIALS

A paragraph of student's writing or use example below
Blank 3″ x 5″ index card or top from a shoe box covered in white paper
The Vertical Elaboration Song (page 42)

Motivation:

Students should strive for vertical elaboration. This type of elaboration lengthens the paper by layering thought.

- Write the following paragraph on a transparency.

> Dinosaurs belong to the lizard family because both are cold blooded and lay eggs. *Dino* means terrible lizard. Each dinosaur has its own name. For example, Tyrant Lizard is the name for Tyrannosaurus and Three Horns is the name for Triceratops.

- Project the paragraph onto the wall. Take the blank index card and place it on the wall where the word terrible is. Pull the card slowly away from the wall and the word will seem to get closer to the students. Students write down the word *terrible* and write another sentence using the word *terrible* in the sentence.

- Choose one of their sentences or the one below to write on the board.

> Dinosaurs were often considered terrible, as some of them were very large and attacked people and smaller dinosaurs.

- As a class, choose another word to pull from that sentence. (A word that sticks in their mind or leaves a strong feeling.) If you used the example sentence guide them to choose *attacked*.

• Take the blank index card and slowly pull the word *attacked* from the wall to focus it for the students.

• Students write another sentence using *attacked* in the sentence.

• Put the following sentence on the board or choose one from the students.

> When attacked, Dinosaurs used their horns, their strength, or their quickness to get away.

• Take the three new sentences and place them after the first sentence so that students can see the elaboration. Our example would now look like this:

> Dinosaurs belong to the lizard family because both are cold blooded and lay eggs. Each dinosaur has its own name. For example, Tyrant Lizard is the name for Tyrannosaurus and Three Horns is the name for Triceratops. *Dino* means terrible. Dinosaurs were often considered terrible as some of them were very large and attacked people and smaller dinosaurs. When attacked, dinosaurs used their horns, their strength, or their quickness to get away.

• When following the first sentence you used, it fits in perfectly and adds vertically to your paragraph.

• Students take out their current piece of writing and choose one sentence to write on another sheet of paper. They should not choose the first or last sentence in the paragraph.

• Students choose a word from this sentence that is important to them, and they write another sentence using that word.

• Students choose a word that is important to them from this new sentence, and they write another sentence.

• Students choose a word that is important to them from this new sentence, and they write a third sentence

• Students insert three new sentences after the sentence that they chose first.

• Students may need to add transitions to make the new sentences flow.

• It is important that you model this technique as per the example above to ensure your students' success.

*Lesson based upon Joyce Armstrong Carroll's *Depth Charging*. See also Prentice Hall, *Writing and Grammar: Communication in Action*. 2000.

MINILESSON #26

Mystery Writing

MATERIALS

Empty detergent box covered orange paper and labeled CLEAN. The letters should be easy to read.
1 sock or sock pattern for each child (mismatched)
Where's My Sock? song (page 42)

Motivation:

• Explain that you have a problem. Your socks are missing.

• Open the detergent box and dump out the mismatched socks. Give each student a sock.

• Tell the students that they need to use their imaginations to help solve the *Missing Sock Mystery*.

• Write the letters C L E A N horizontally on the board, leaving space for the explanatory word or words.

    C=Creative,   L=Lively,   E=Elaboration,   A=Adjectives, Adverbs, Alliteration
N=Nothing but your best

• Point to each letter in the word CLEAN, explaining the meaning represented by each letter.

• Explain that their writing should contain all of the above to solve the mystery.

• Sing *Where's My Sock?*
• Students write the *Missing Sock Mystery*.
• Encourage students to be CLEAN in their writing.

ELEMENTARY MINILESSONS

#21

More Attractive Adjectives

MATERIALS

Many Luscious Lollipops, Ruth Heller
Lollipop pattern (I use the bottom of a glass for a circle.)
Popsicle stick for each student
Colorful wrapping paper (I use swirled tissue paper.)
White poster board or tag board

Motivation:

• Read *Many Luscious Lollipops* and discuss the adjectives.
If possible, have enough books to pass out to groups of three or four students.

• Have each child cut out a circle from both tag board and wrapping paper.

• Glue the circles together.

• Tape the popsicle stick to the back of the tag board.

• Students then search through the book and write at least ten adjectives on their lollipop that they could use in their writing.

• Using their luscious lollipop, the students look at their current piece of writing and add at least three adjectives.

• Helpful Hint: Remind students to find out what the adjective means before using it.

ELEMENTARY MINILESSONS

MINILESSON #28 Adjective Ann and Andy

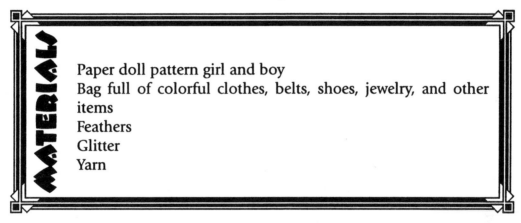

MATERIALS

Paper doll pattern girl and boy
Bag full of colorful clothes, belts, shoes, jewelry, and other items
Feathers
Glitter
Yarn

Motivation:

• Invite a volunteer to be your Adjective Ann or Adjective Andy.

• Take him/her out of the classroom and dress in clothes, belts, shoes, and jewelry. Sponge rollers in the hair add a nice touch.

• Bring Adjective Ann or Andy to the front of the classroom.

• As a class, brainstorm as many adjectives as you can to describe what you see.

• Guide the students to discover as many as imaginable. Stretch them to choose words other than just *big, little, pretty,* or *nice.*

• Have the students choose a girl or boy paper doll pattern.

• Students create their own Adjective Ann or Andy using markers, crayons or colored pencils, feathers. glitter, and yarn.

• Students write a description of their Adjective Ann or Andy.

• Students share their writing while a friend holds up their picture.

• Class adds anything the student forgot.

    For example, *You said two eyes. What color were they? You forgot her ears, uh oh!*

• Encourage students to go back to their current piece of writing and add adjectives.

ELEMENTARY MINILESSONS

Students can create their own Adjective Andy and Ann.

ELEMENTARY MINILESSONS

MINILESSON

#29 Sending Letters

MATERIALS

Copy of *The Parts of a Letter* song (page 43)
One of the books from the list of books that contain let-ters(See list on page 38 and bibliography page 56.)
Cereal box puzzles.

Motivation:

• Read the book that was chosen.
• Discuss the parts of a letter and write them on the chalkboard or markerboard.
• Show the students examples of letters. Discuss the parts of each letter.
• Sing *The Parts of a Letter* song.
• Distribute cereal box puzzles. Students put puzzles together reinforcing the parts of a letter.
• As a class, write a letter to the custodians thanking them for keeping the classroom neat. Model using the correct parts of a letter.
• Students write a thank you letter to a person of their choice.
• An envelope template can be used to encourage students to write letters. Students trace the pattern on wrapping paper, and cut it out. Students write their thank you letters on the white side of the paper, fold to create an envelope. Address it and send the letter!

ELEMENTARY MINILESSONS

A list of books that can be used in your letter writing lessons (see bibliography for complete citation):

Letters From Rifka, Karen Hesse
The Lettuce Leaf Birthday Letter, Linda Taylor
Angel's Mother's Boyfriend, Judy Delton*
A Letter to the King, Leong Va
Dear Mr. Blueberry, James Simon
Thank You Santa, Margaret Wild
Dear Mr. Henshaw, Beverly Clearly*
Dear Brother, Frank Asch
Messages in the Mailbox How to Write a Letter, Loreen Leedy
The Mailbox Trick, Scott Corbett*
Sea Swan, Kathryn Lasky
What to do When Your Mom or Dad Say... "Write to Grandma!", Joy Wilt Berry:
The Jolly Postman, Jean and Allan Ahlsberg
Utterly Yours, Booker Jones, Betsy Puffy*
* chapter book

Puzzle Directions:

On the back of the cover write a letter. Next, cut the letter into ten pieces creating a puzzle. Place each puzzle in an envelope. Label the puzzle, stating who the letter is to. For example—envelope 1—Dear Miss Piggy.)

Model Letter for Cereal box Puzzle:

November 3, 1999
Dear Miss Piggy,

I hope you are feeling well and that you are taking care of yourself. I just want to

thank you for sending me your latest CD. Mrs. Ramos and I have enjoyed it. She has shared

it with the students at Steubing Elementary and they have enjoyed it as well. I am always

inspired by your voice. I hope to be able to visit you some day soon.

Hogs and Kisses,

Petunia P. Pig

(This letter is written on the back of a cereal cover and cut apart to create a puzzle. Students put the puzzles together as they study the parts of a letter!)

Elaboration

(To the tune of the *Mickey Mouse March*)

E-L-A-B-O-R-A-T-I-O-N (Spell the word.)
Elaboration is the way to make your writing exciting every day.
E-L-A-B-O-R-A-T-I-O-N
Now take the cat and make it fat, black as night, slinking slowly , causing mice fright.
E-L-A-B-O-R-A-T-I-O-N
Elaboration can cause sensation use it many ways each and every day.
Now take a pig, wearing a red wig singing folk songs and doing and Irish jig.
E-L-A-B-O-R-A-T-I-O-N
Elaboration is the way to make your writing exciting every day.
E-L-A-B-O-R-A-T-I-O-N
Elaboration!!!!

EVERYBODY CLOCK!

(To the tune of the *Let's Go to the Hop*) Clocking is a proofreading/editing technique. There are complete directions in the *Acts of Teaching*, Carroll & Wilson, 282-284.

This song facilitates clocking. I mainly use the chorus. Sometimes I just play the chorus and the students clock. I later wrote the verses, but it is a lot of singing!

Chorus:
Everybody clock (clap clap clap clap).
Everybody clock (clap clap clap clap).
We want to know what our friends wrote so
Everybody clock (clap clap clap clap)

Verse 1:
Is there a title on the top? Everybody check, make sure that it's capitalized.
Everybody check. Check for the title at the top and remember to initial please.
(Give them time to do this and then sing the chorus, signaling them to exchange papers and move!)

Verse 2:
Now it's time to check and see if you used end marks. Remember to check for commas, periods, question and exclamation marks. Please check for all of these, remember to initial please. (Give time and go back to the chorus.)

Verse 3:

Spelling is a difficult thing so let's carefully check. Read backwards in a slow manner and check each letter please. Do your very best, to your best ability!

(Give time and go back to the chorus.)

One more time spelling check please and remember to go slow.

This job is an important one, so take your time, please.

(Give time and go back to the chorus.)

There's so much more than we can clock for so listen carefully!

Remember to clock when you hear the keys play.

Everybody Clock!

Writing the _____ Way!

(To the tune of *Rock Around the Clock*)

Prewrite...
    Write...
        Revise...
            Edit...
                Publish...

Prewrite...
    Write...
        Revise...
            Edit...
                Publish... (Repeat a third time.)

We're gonna write... and write... and write some more.

When the school bell rings and announcements start,

We listen with all our heart,

Because in just a minute or more,

We're gonna write...and write...and write galore!

We're learning to write the _____ way today..ay..ay..ay..ay...ay.

Each and every single day,

Something written will come your way.

A book, a check, a note, or a sign...something's written all the time.

Yes, everybody really has to learn to write...ite...ite...ite...ite...ite...ite.

And did you know that football players write?

They have charts and graphs to get those plays just right.

And rock stars do, yes they write too.

ELEMENTARY MINILESSONS

Music and lyrics to keep their songs in tune.
Yes, everybody really has to learn to write...ite...ite...ite...ite...ite...ite.

So, learn the basics then elaborate and keep your skills up to date.
Because an apple a day may keep the doctor away,
But a well written page may pay the bills someday.
Yes, everybody really has to learn to write...ite...ite...ite...ite...ite...ite.
Yes, everybody really has to learn to write...ite...ite...ite...ite...ite...ite.
YEAH!!

The How To Song

(To the tune of the verse section of the *Hokey Poky*)

You put your sequence words in
You never leave them out!
You put your sequence words in
And you mix them all about.
You organize your steps never leaving details out
That's what it's all about!
You give it to a friend.
And he reads it out loud.
He tries all your steps.
And you should be proud.
He creates what you wanted with your organized plan.
That's what it's all about!
You did a How To!
You did a How To!
Like the part that goes Hokey Poky!

I've Got the Whole Story in My Hand

(To the tune of *He's Got the Whole World in His Hands*)

I've got the whole story in my hand.
I've got the whole story in my hand.
I've got the whole story in my hand.
I've got the whole story in my hand.
I've got characters that tell who or what.
A setting that tells me where and when.

A problem that show there is trouble.
I've got the whole story in my hand.

There are may events telling what happens.
An ending that tells how the problem is solved.
I've got lots of elaboration in my story!
I've got the whole story in my hand.

The Vertical Elaboration Song

(To the tune of *Ten Little Indians*)

Take a sentence from your paragraph, not the first and not the last.
Choose one word from that sentence that is important to you.
Write a sentence using that word, write a sentence using that word. We are making your paragraph the best it can be.

Now take that sentence and choose another word. Now take that sentence and choose another word. Write another sentence using that word. We are making your paragraph better.
One last time choose another word and make a sentence using that word. Your paragraph will thank you. You made it the best that it can be.
Now place these sentences back in your paragraph, right after the first sentence that you chose. You just elaborated vertically, give yourself a pat on the back.

Where's My Sock song

(To the tune of *Are You Sleeping Brother John?*)

Where's my sneaker?
Where's my sneaker?
Where's my sock?
Where's my sock?
I have looked most everywhere.
I can't find them anywhere.
Frozen toes.
Frozen toes.

The Parts of a Letter

(To the tune of *Head, Shoulders, Knees and Toes*)

Heading, Greeting, Body, Closing, Signature
Heading, Greeting, Body, Closing, Signature
Now I know the Parts of a Letter
Heading, Greeting, Body, Closing, Signature

This is a short song to aid in teaching the parts of a letter. There are simple actions to go with the song.
Touch your head on Heading.
Touch your shoulders on Greeting.
Touch you waist on Body.
Touch you knees on Closing.
Touch your toes on Signature.
Point to your eye on I.
Point to your nose on Know.
Point with fingers to form letters on Parts of a Letter.

ELEMENTARY MINILESSONS

MUSICAL READING, WRITING CONNECTION

When reading a picture book to students it is effective to give them a concrete object (artifact) that connects them to the story. This artifact is theirs to keep and use as a motivator when they write.

Time Flies, Eric Rohmann

Artifact: Feather

Music: Strauss 2001 from the Classical Thunder CD

Turn pages of the book as the music plays. Practice turning the pages to meet the dramatic music. Later act out the story using feathers. Brainstorm what students could write about. List all possibilities. Students choose one to write about.

Kat Kong, Dav Pilkey

Artifact: Cat or mouse sticker

Music: Cat and Mouse, Aaron Copeland

Turn pages of the book as the music plays. Later read the story. Students stick their sticker on a sheet of 8 1/2 x 11 paper. Students draw a picture around their sticker. Students write a new ending or new section to the original story.

Tuesday, David Wiesner

Artifact: Paper plate (for a lily pad) Students can color the plate green and cut a triangular slit into the plate to create a lily pad.

Music: Flight of the Valkyries, Wagner

Turn the pages of the book as the music plays. Students sit on paper plate lily pads as the music plays. The second time the students move as the frogs do in the book. Then they can write about their adventures.

Stella and Roy, Ashley Wolff

A brother and sister race their toy bikes to a surprising ending.

Or

Bonnie Blair a Winning Edge, Bonnie Blair with Greg Brown

Bonnie Blair is an Olympic speed skater.

Or

Super Grandpa, David M. Schwartz

Grandpa wants to be in a bicycle race, but they say he is too old. He races anyway and wins.

Artifact: First Place ribbon or *I Am Special* ribbon

Music: William Tell Overture, Rossini

Choose a book from the examples above. Turn the pages as the music plays. You may want to read the book later. Pass out the ribbons (artifacts). Students write why they are winners.

SOME BRIEF REMARKS ABOUT WRITING

The Writing Process

Publishing/Sharing: Classrooms usually have available a variety of materials for publishing using techniques the teacher has presented during minilessons. The workshop functions much more efficiently when children can manage independently the publication stage of the process. Teachers may also set up a system for the sharing of writing. Sometimes students celebrate the completion of stories, reading from an Author's Chair, other times they seek out their classmates' responses to work in progress. An author's chair is a chair designated for students to sit in when they share their reading. The chair can be elaborate as a director's chair with stenciled letters stating - Author's chair - or as simple as a stool. It is reserved for the sharing of writing.

Criteria for Finished Writing
The writing process is complete, presentable and well organized.
The writing is free of spelling and usage errors.
The writing flows.
The writing is appropriate for the audience.
The purpose is fulfilled.

CLOCKING

Clocking is a technique used on completed writing to make a final check for specific criteria. Students can make any necessary changes on the final copy. Examples of grade-level criteria are as follows:

Grade:	Clock For:
Kinder	Name Title
1st Grade	Name Title Capital Letters End Marks Spelling
2nd Grade	Name Title Capital Letters End Marks Spelling Sentence Structure (run-ons, fragments, subject-verb agreement)

SOME BRIEF REMARKS ABOUT WRITING

3rd Grade
and
4th Grade
and
5th Grade
	Name
	Title
	Capital Letters
	End Marks
	Spelling
	Sentence Structure
	(run-ons, fragments,
	     subject-verb agreement)
	adding whatever you teach,
	     such as to, too and two,
	     there/their/they're
	or *be* verbs: am, is, are, was, were,
	     be, being, been.

Clocking Procedure:

1. Students are arranged in two circles, one inside the other. Inner circle faces outward and outer circle faces inward so that one paired students face each other around the circle. Another arrangement would be to place students in two rows facing each other. This is called digital clocking. Students begin with their final copy of their own writing with a clocking sheet on top. They trade their writing and clocking sheet for their partner's writing and clocking sheet.

2. Students sign or initial next to each criterion they are checking on the clocking sheet

3. They check the paper for that specific criterion.

4. After checking, the students mark the clocking sheet to show whether or not the criterion was correct. Once all students have completed checking the criterion they return the writing and clocking sheet to their partner. Then they can move to the next spot. Students in the outer circle move one space to the right (like the hands of a clock, hence the name) so that they will have a new partner for checking the next criterion. If the students are arranged in two rows, each person in one row moves one space to the right, and the student at the end goes to the beginning of the row.

Once settled, students repeat steps until all the criteria have been checked. After clocking is completed, students make corrections on their final copy.

ELEMENTARY MINILESSONS

How to create the *Crackle and Crunch Box*

1. Cover the Box with white paper.

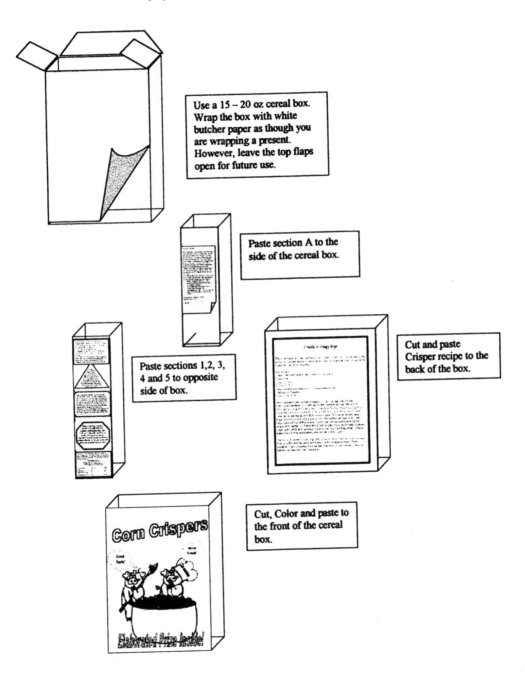

Use a 15 – 20 oz cereal box. Wrap the box with white butcher paper as though you are wrapping a present. However, leave the top flaps open for future use.

Paste section A to the side of the cereal box.

Paste sections 1,2, 3, 4 and 5 to opposite side of box.

Cut and paste Crisper recipe to the back of the box.

Cut, Color and paste to the front of the cereal box.

Corn Crispers
Hi, I'm Crackle!
I'm Crunch!
Sounds Great!
Elaborated Prize Inside!

ELEMENTARY MINILESSONS

Side panels

Cut and Paste Section

A.

Cut and paste to the side of box.

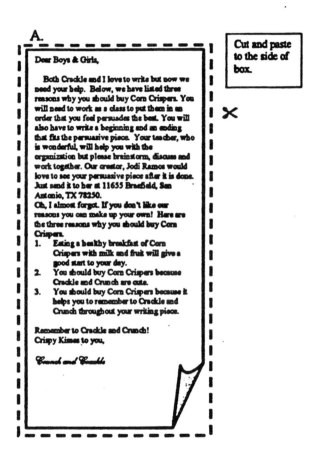

Dear Boys & Girls,

Both Crackle and I love to write but now we need your help. Below, we have listed three reasons why you should buy Corn Crispers. You will need to work as a class to put them in an order that you feel persuades the best. You will also have to write a beginning and an ending that fits the persuasive piece. Your teacher, who is wonderful, will help you with the organization but please brainstorm, discuss and work together. Our creator, Jodi Ramos would love to see your persuasive piece after it is done. Just send it to her at 11655 Braefield, San Antonio, TX 78250.

Oh, I almost forgot. If you don't like our reasons you can make up your own! Here are the three reasons why you should buy Corn Crispers.

1. Eating a healthy breakfast of Corn Crispers with milk and fruit will give a good start to your day.
2. You should buy Corn Crispers because Crackle and Crunch are cute.
3. You should buy Corn Crispers because it helps you to remember to Crackle and Crunch throughout your writing piece.

Remember to Crackle and Crunch!
Crispy Kisses to you,

Crunch and Crackle

1.

Cut and paste to the side of the cereal box.

Learning to eat a healthy breakfast should start when you are young. My mother always fed me a nutritious breakfast; Corn Crispers, skim milk, a bowl of fresh fruit, and orange juice. Days that I was in a hurry I had to grab a quick dry bowl of cereal but my mom thought milk was important. In the paragraphs below, I compare and contrast the good and bad about eating cereal without milk.

2.

Cut and paste under the square to the side of the cereal box.

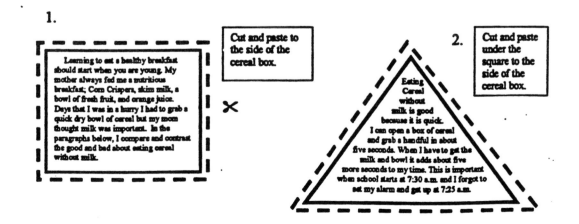

Eating Cereal without milk is good because it is quick. I can open a box of cereal and grab a handful in about five seconds. When I have to get the milk and bowl it adds about five more seconds to my time. This is important when school starts at 7:30 a.m. and I forgot to set my alarm and got up at 7:25 a.m.

ELEMENTARY MINILESSONS

Eating cereal without out milk is good because there aren't any dishes to wash. I close the box tightly so the cereal doesn't get stale and eat it out of my hand. When I am done I lick my hand clean. I don't have to turn the water on, or get the soap and rag. The licking of my hand saves my hands from being stuck in sudsy water. Sure, we have a dishwasher but then you have to take out the detergent and pour it into the dispenser. Then, turn on the dishwasher and wait around until it is done to put the bowl neatly away. My mom does not like bowls sitting out on the counter. Remember that all takes time and I don't have much when I wake up late.

3.

Cut and paste under the triangle shape on the side of the box.

4.

Eating cereal without milk is good because milk adds more sodium to your morning meal. One half cup of skim milk contributes an additional 65mg of sodium (salt). I am always hearing on television how bad sodium is for you. So If I can cut out a few grams here and there, it is a good idea.

Cut and paste under the rectangle shape on the side of the box.

5.

I did tell you that I would mention the bad things about eating cereal without milk. I really ran out of space.
Please brainstorm as a class and write down why it is bad to eat cereal without milk. I wrote down a few facts to start you along.

Nutrition Facts
Serving Size 11/4 Cup (33g/1.2 oz.)
Serving Size per Package About 12

Per Serving	Cereal	With Milk
Calories	120	160
Total Fat 0%	0%	0%
Potassium 40 mg	1%	7%
Carbohydrate 29g	10%	11%

Cut and paste under the octagon shape to the side of the cereal box.

Crackle's Crispy Pops

When I get hungry and want something to eat, I make Crackle pops. They are named after me but you can make them too. Follow the directions below and make sure you have all the ingredients right at your fingertips.

You will need:
1 large cookie sheet sprayed with vegetable cooking spray
1 large bowl
1 large saucepan
20 Popsicle sticks
4 cups miniature marshmallows or 40 regular marshmallows
3 tablespoons margarine
6 cups crispy cereal

With your parent's help, melt the margarine in a large saucepan over low heat. Next, add the marshmallows slowly and stir them until they are completely melted. After, they are completely melted, remove them from the stove. Place them on another burner that is not on or a potholder. Now, you will need to pour the six cups of crispy cereal into the pan and stir until all the cereal is coated. This is the tricky part, using a baggie or a piece of waxed paper pick of some of the mixture and make a ball (a little larger than a golf ball) with your hand. Place the ball onto the cooking sheet that you sprayed with vegetable oil. Flatten the ball with the palm of your hand to make a pancake shape. Lastly, gently push one Popsicle stick in to the end of the flattened ball. Continue making balls of cereal and flattening them until the mixture is gone.

You have now created a Crackle Pop, well actually you have created about 20 crackle pops. Now, go to the phone and invite your friends over for a crackling good time. Please remember to ask your parents if you can first. Remember, to give everyone a recipe so that they can make their own Crackle pops.

Cut and paste to the
back of the box.

ELEMENTARY MINILESSONS

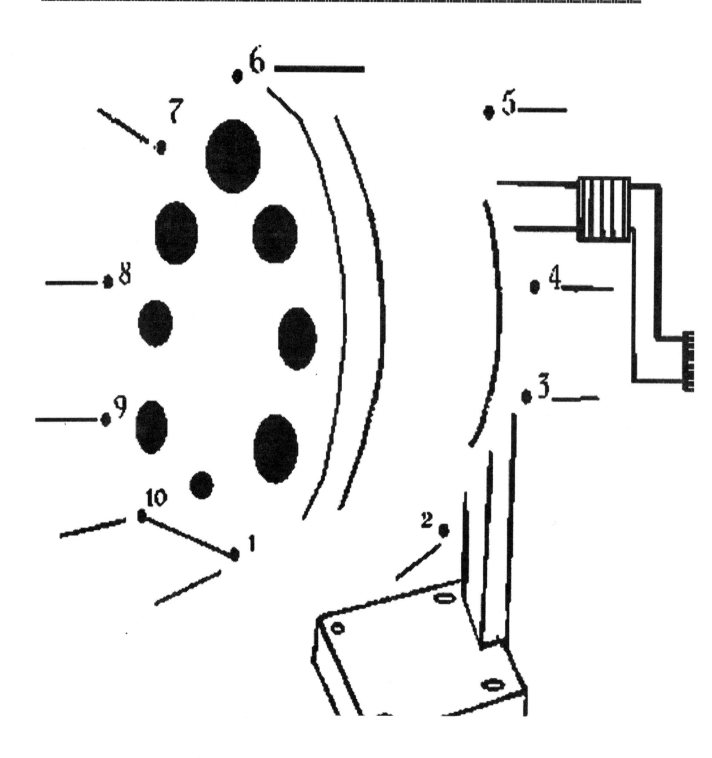

ELEMENTARY MINILESSONS

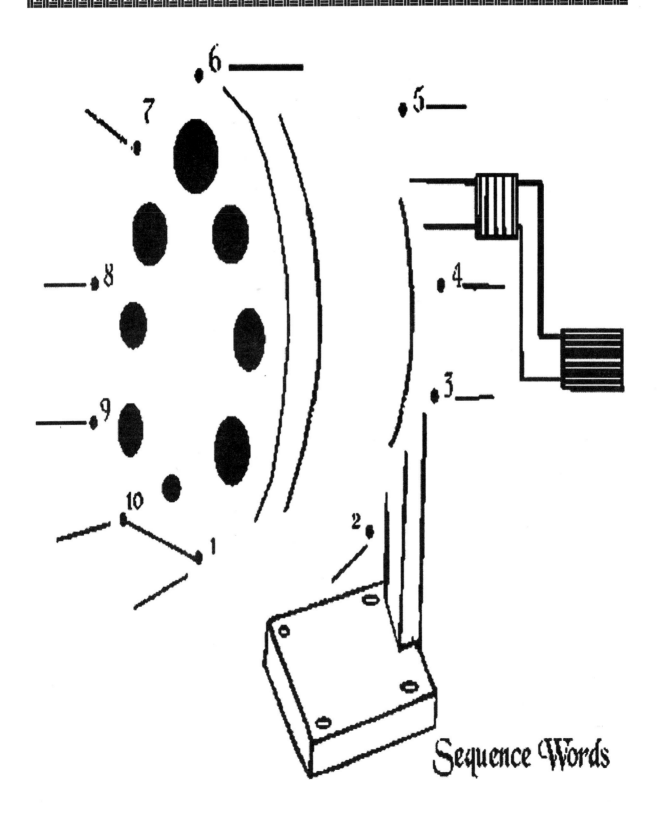

Sequence Words

ELEMENTARY MINILESSONS

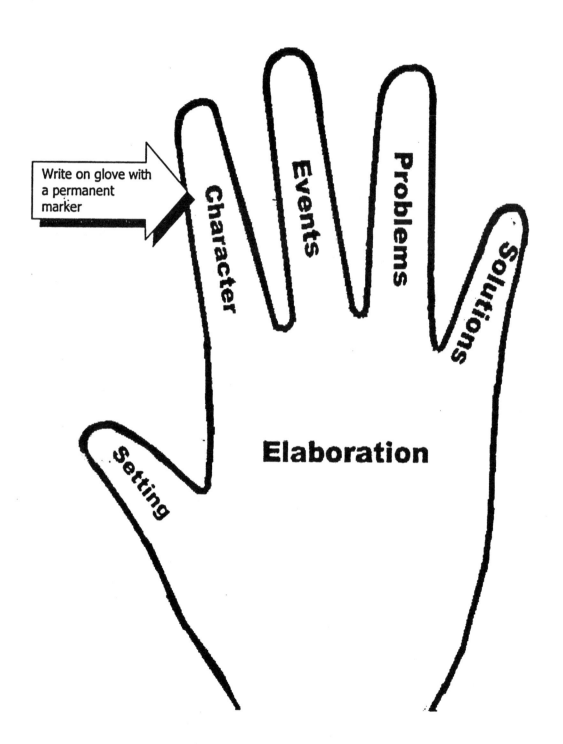

Write on glove with a permanent marker

Character

Events

Problems

Solutions

Setting

Elaboration

Copy and cut out the cards for The Elaboration Game.

The Elaboration Game

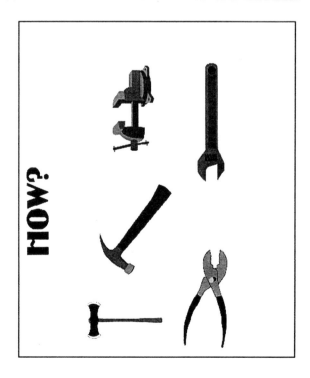

Copy and cut out the cards for The Elaboration Game.

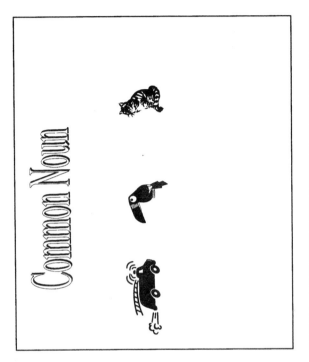

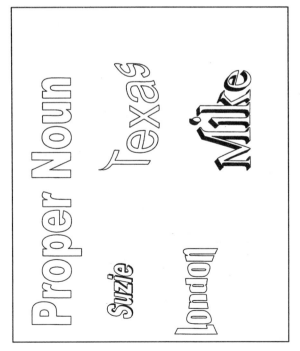

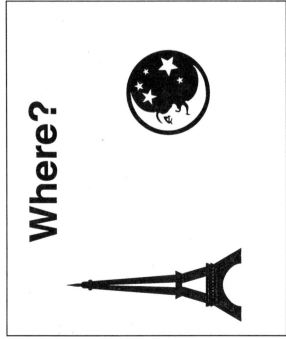

ELEMENTARY MINILESSONS

Copy and cut out the cards for The Elaboration Game.

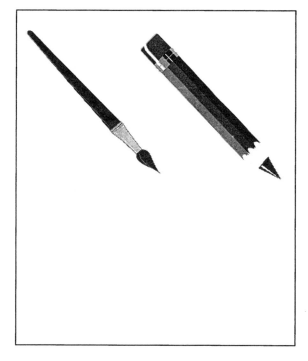

Copy and cut out the cards for The Elaboration Game.

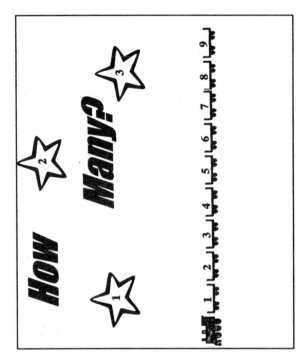

Asch,Frank and Vldimir Vagin. *Dear Brother.New York:* Scholastic,1992.

Berry, Joy Wilt. *What to do when your mom or dad says "Behave in public!"* Chicago: Childrens Press,1987.

Carroll,Joyce Armstrong and Edward E. Wilson. *Acts of teaching: how to teach writing.* Englewood,CO: Teacher Ideas Press, 1993.

Carlson, Nancy L. *How to lose all your friends.* New York: Puffin Books, 1997.

Cleary,Beverly. *Dear Mr. Henshaw.* New York: Avon, 1996.

Corbett,Scott. *The mailbox trick.* New York: Scholastic, 1961.

Delton,Judy. *Angels's mother's boyfriend.* Boston,Mass.: Houghton Mifflin, 1986.

Duffey,Betsy. *Utterly yours, Booker Jones.* New York: Viking, 1995.

Heller,Ruth. *Many Luscious Lollipops-a Book About Adjectives.* New York: Scholastic, 1989.

Hesse,Karen. *Letters from Rifka.* New York: H. Holt, 1992

Hoban,Tana. *Exactly the opposite.* New York: Greenwillow Books, 1997 1990.

Hoban, Tana. *Look again!* New York: Macmillan, 1971.

James,Simon. *Dear Mr. Blueberry.* New York: McElderry, 1991.

Lasky, Kathryn. *Sea Swan.* New York: Macmillan, 1988.

Leedy, Loreen. *Mesaages in the mailbox: how to write a letter.* New York: Holiday House, 1991.

Nixon, Joan Lowery . *If you were a writer.* New York: Aladdin Paperbacks,1995.

Oppenheim, Joanne. *"Uh-oh!" said the crow.* Gareth Stevens, 1997.

Parish, Peggy. *Amelia Bedelia.* New York: Harper Arco Iris, 1996.

Pelham,David. *The Sensational Samburger.* New York: Dutton Children's Press,1995

Rambeck,Richard. *Bonnie Blair.* Plymouth, MN: Child's World, 1996.

Rohmann, Eric. *Time flies.* New York: Crown, 1994.

Schwarts, David M. *Supergrandpa.* New York: Lothrop, 1991.

Taylor,Linda. *The lettuce leaf birthday letter.* New York: Dial Books for Young Readers, 1995.

Va, Leong. *A letter to the king.* New York: HarperCollins, 1991.

Van Allsburg, Chris. *The wreck of the Zephyr.* Boston: Houghton Mifflin, 1983.

Van Allsburg, Chris. *Z was zapped.* Boston: Houghton Mifflin, 1987.

Wiesner, David. *Tuesday.* SRA/McGraw-Hill, 1992.

Wild,Margaret. *Thank you Santa.* Scholastic, 1992.

Wolf, Ashley, *Stella and Roy.* New York: Penguin, 1993.